RACE TO THE POLE

MEREDITH HOOPER

Hodder
Children's
Books

A ooks

**To Warren Zapol, Antarctic scientist,
and Guy Guthridge, Antarctic enabler.**

Text copyright 2002 © Meredith Hooper
First published by Hodder Children's Books 2002
This edition published in 2007

Picture 1:	© Scott Polar Research Institute, University of Cambridge
Picture 2:	© Dulwich College, reproduced by kind permission of Dulwich College
Picture 3:	© reproduced by permission of the Norwegian Folk Museum
Picture 4:	© reproduced by permission of the National Library of Norway, Oslo Division, Picture Collection
Pictures 5 & 6:	© Scott Polar Research Institute, University of Cambridge
Pictures 7 & 8:	© reproduced by permission of the National Library of Norway, Oslo Division, Picture Collection
Cover pictures:	© Scott Polar Research Institute, University of Cambridge

The right of Meredith Hooper to be identified as the author of the work has been asserted by her in accordance with the Copyright, Designs and Patents Act 1988.

1

A catalogue record for this book is available from the British Library.

0 0 MAR 2017

ISBN-13: 978 0 340 94527 8

Typeset in Bembo by Avon DataSet Ltd, Bidford on Avon, Warwickshire

Printed in the UK by CPI Bookmarque, Croydon, CR0 4TD

The paper and board used in this paperback by Hodder Children's Books are natural recyclable products made from wood grown in sustainable forests. The manufacturing processes conform to the environmental regulations of the country of origin.

Hodder Children's Books
a division of Hachette Children's Books
338 Euston Road, London NW1 3BH
An Hachette Livre UK company

0 0 MAR 2017

Contents

The men in this book were obsessed with the distances they had to travel. How far was it to the South Pole? How much further to the nearest depot of food and fuel, or the final safety of their base hut? In Antarctica, explorers thought in nautical miles; just as sailors do at sea, and pilots in the air. In telling their stories, this book uses the measurements the explorers used. One hundred nautical miles equals approximately 115 statute miles, or 185 kilometres. There is more information about measuring distance on page 111–112.

Meredith Hooper has written over fifty books, and eight of her most recent titles are about the huge continent at the bottom of the world. She has travelled south with the Australian National Antarctic Research Expeditions, and the US National Science Foundation Artists & Writers Program. In 2000 she was awarded the US Antarctica Service Medal. Meredith Hooper writes: 'Hackle, the rat hero of my novel *The Pole-seekers*, describes Antarctica: "It had entered our souls," he says. "It would mark us for ever." I think that happened to the explorers who dreamt of standing at the South Pole. It can happen to people who go to Antarctica today. I know that Antarctica has a great grip on my imagination. It affects for ever the way I think about the world.'

Chapter 1

THE GREAT PRIZE

WHO will get to the South Pole first? There can be only one winner.

Nobody has got to the North Pole either. The North Pole is in an ice-filled sea, ringed by land.

But no one even knows if the South Pole is on land or sea. A vast ocean heaves continually around the bottom of the world, whipped by storms. Enormous icebergs float deep in the freezing water. Every winter, shifting, grinding ice floes form across the ocean's surface. Far to the south, bits of coastline have been discovered, hints that a huge continent might lie beyond. Only seals, penguins and sea birds seem to use these ice-bound shores. Nothing grows on the bare, shattered rocks, except a few scraps of toe-high grass, and patches of lichens and moss. No land-living animals seem to live here, or any native people.

So why search for the South Pole?

What drives the contestants?

The restless excitement of exploring drives them. The thrill of the unknown. There aren't many undiscovered places left in the world. But in Antarctica everything waits, barely touched.

Powerful ambition drives them. The Pole has yet to be bagged. Someone will put his name to it. That person will be honoured, famous, remembered for ever.

Patriotism drives them. Which nation will achieve this great goal? The British believe that it should be them.

FIRE AND ICE

A sheer cliff of ice rises out of the sea, stretching into the distance, massive, forbidding. What lies behind this wall of ice? Even from the crow's nest high on a ship's mast, it's impossible to see. The British call it the Great Barrier. Somewhere beyond, far to the south, lies the South Pole.

A British naval captain is the first to see the wall of ice. In 1841, James Clark Ross sailed further south than anyone had ever been, discovering a new coast, with massive mountain ranges and mighty glaciers. Ross was astonished to find a snow-covered volcano spewing out smoke and flames. He called it Mount Erebus after his ship. The land with the volcano was later named Ross Island, and the sea he sailed over, the Ross Sea. Much later, the Great Barrier became known as the Ross Ice Shelf.

The first explorers managed to land on the Barrier in 1900. Eagerly they looked south, and saw a great plain of ice stretching endlessly into the distance. Stupendous. Utterly barren. Utterly still. Sending, said one, 'an indefinable sense of dread to the heart'. They set off south with their dog sledge for a couple of hours, before they had to turn back to their ship. But they'd got closer to the Pole than anyone else.

It is here, on the great ice plain – the Barrier – that the race to the Pole will be played out.

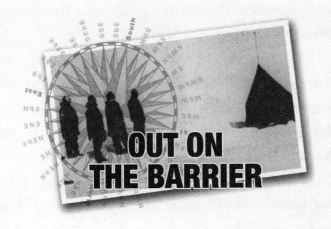

OUT ON THE BARRIER

IT'S early summer. Sunday 2 November 1902. Cold and windy.

Three men begin travelling south.

Commander Robert Falcon Scott, aged thirty-four, leader of the British National Antarctic Expedition. Royal Navy officer.

Lieutenant Ernest Shackleton, aged twenty-eight, officer in the British Merchant Navy.

Dr Edward Wilson, aged thirty, recently qualified medical doctor.

For nearly a year, their ship *Discovery* has been frozen into the sea at the edge of Ross Island, below the volcano Mount Erebus. Now the three men are walking into the absolutely unknown, into an icy desert. Nineteen dogs will help them pull five sledges across the Barrier.

The British National Antarctic Expedition is here to make geographical discoveries, and carry out scientific work. The ultimate achievement would be the South Pole. No one is saying that out loud. But it's the dream.

The Pole is 730 miles due south. It's easy to know how far. It's easy to know the right direction. The South Pole is where all the lines of longitude meet in a single point, at the bottom of the world. It's where the Earth turns on its axis. It's an idea. But it's also a fact of geography. The South Pole is a real, measurable, tiny spot on the planet. It's the place where – when you finally reach it – every direction points to the north.

Scott, Shackleton and Wilson head south over the huge, empty plain of ice that stretches on, glittering, featureless. As they trudge, they discover, away to their right, a new range of mountains with sharp, ice-clenched peaks. Their attempt to get the dogs to pull their sledges fails dismally. The dogs weaken and die. Some are killed to feed the others. The three men harness themselves to their sledges and drag them along.

British polar explorers believe in 'man-hauling', in using humans as pack animals. There's nothing to equal the honest use of your own legs, Scott says. Harnessing men to sledges is a British tradition that began with explorers in the Arctic.

On the last day of December they turn back. Terribly hungry. Defeated by distance, ignorance, inexperience. Scott and Shackleton's increasing dislike of each other breaks out in quarrelling. To save weight, Scott orders the skis to be thrown away. Wilson persuades him to keep one pair for emergencies.

All are suffering symptoms of the dreadful disease, scurvy. But from the middle of January, Shackleton becomes worryingly ill, too weak to help pull the sledges, or do camp work. He manages to keep going, using the only pair of skis to support his weight on the breaking crust of snow.

The men only just make it back. Thin, sick, exhausted. Faces scarred by frostbite, burnt like old boots by the glaring sun. They've travelled for ninety-three days. They've got 227 miles further south than anyone else. But nowhere near the Pole.

A relief ship has arrived from England. Scott orders Shackleton on board, to be invalided home.

Scott, and most of his men, will stay on in Antarctica for another year of exploring.

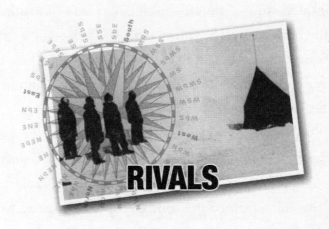

Chapter 4

RIVALS

S HACKLETON returns to England burning with ambition. He wants to rescue his reputation from the shame of being sent home as unfit. He wants to prove that he is a better man than Scott. He longs to go on another expedition. But, most powerfully, he longs to get to the Pole. To conquer it. To be first.

Scott returns to England. He publishes an excellently written book about the *Discovery* expedition. In his book Scott appears as modest and gentle-manly, battling against the Fates. Their southern journey failed, he says, because the dogs failed; and because Shackleton broke down completely on the way back.

Shackleton never forgives Scott for what he considers to be public humiliation and untruths. Somehow – by the power of his personality, by talking, and persuading – he organises his own private expedition, the British Antarctic Expedition. International interest in the Antarctic is growing.

Shackleton hasn't nearly enough money for his expedition. He rushes the planning. He buys *Nimrod*, an old Norwegian ship used for seal hunting, stinking of seal-oil, a fifth of the tonnage of Scott's specially-built expedition ship the *Discovery*. He chooses adventurous men to accompany him. *Nimrod* will unload expedition members and their supplies at a base camp in Antarctica, then escape from the winter ice and sail north to New Zealand. Shackleton plans to get some science done, and some exploring. But above everything, he's going to get the Pole.

The newspapers are behind him. They want the Pole for Britain. Shackleton's men feel proud, excited, full of hope.

Scott is furious. He is equally determined, equally ambitious. He is convinced that he has the right to try for the Pole before all others. It's his. He will get it, for himself, and for his country. He must. It's his life's work.

But his fury can't be public. Privately, Scott and Shackleton argue. Scott claims exclusive rights to 'his' part of Antarctica and forbids Shackleton to go anywhere near a large area including Ross Island. Shackleton cannot use the route to the Pole he pioneered with Scott and Wilson – that would be 'poaching', says Scott. He has to start from somewhere else.

Shackleton promises. He has to.

Chapter 5

A CAR AND SOME PONIES

INLAND, away from the coast, Antarctica provides not one shred of food. Not one drop of water. Scott, Shackleton and Wilson existed on starvation rations during their southern journey. That journey taught Shackleton a lot about the difficulties of pole-seeking.

He and the two or three men he chooses to go with him to the Pole will have to carry every single thing they will need on the journey. Every mouthful of food. Enough fuel for cooking, and to melt snow to make water. Thick, warm sleeping bags to keep them alive in the terrible cold. Spare sets of clothes. Tents, boots, lamps, matches, rope, compasses, shovels.

Enough to take them all the way to the Pole, and all the way back. Crucially, Shackleton must solve the problem of how to transport these heavy loads.

The Norwegians are experienced in polar travelling, and Shackleton asks their most famous explorer, Fridtjof Nansen, for advice. He goes to Norway, as Scott did before him, to buy kit: some wolfskin mitts; sleeping bags made of reindeer fur; boots like the Lapps wear, lined with special dry grass to absorb sweat; wooden sledges; a few pairs of skis.

The Norwegians have no doubt about the most efficient way to travel over ice and snow, the best way to carry the weight of supplies. Use skis. Use dogs. In Norway, skiing has long been a way for people to get around, but now it's changing fast into a modern sport. Equipment is improving rapidly. The Norwegians try to persuade Shackleton to use skis. They advise him to use teams of thick-coated, broad-chested husky dogs from the shores of Alaska and Greenland to pull the heavy sledges.

Scott, on Norwegian advice, took skis and dogs on the *Discovery* expedition. But the British didn't know how to use the long heavy skis properly. They didn't understand how to use dogs, or get them to work efficiently. Skiing needs lots of training and practice. Dog-driving requires real skill and good technique.

Shackleton doesn't like skis and he doesn't trust dogs. He does trust men hauling their own loads, walking on their own two feet. But he comes up with some new ideas. He will take ponies – sturdy little animals from Manchuria, in northern China. He's heard that they do well in the snow. And he will take the very latest invention – a motor car, specially adapted to travel over snow and ice. It might allow him to 'sprint' to the Pole, he says. The car will haul the sledges across the great ice plain. If it fails, the ponies will take over.

The car needs fuel, and an engineer who understands how to fix it. Ponies are herbivores, and there's nothing for them to eat in Antarctica. Their bulky food must be carried. Skis, and the runners of sledges, distribute weight evenly over the snow surface. That is their great advantage. Ponies are heavy animals. All their weight bears down on four sharp hooves.

The Norwegians are astonished. But Shackleton is convinced. He has to get heavy supplies south to use on the march, and this is the way he will do it.

Chapter 6

SHACKLETON'S HUT

WINTER 1908. Cape Royds, Ross Island, Antarctica. Shackleton's hut shakes and quivers in the howling winds.

Strong wire cables over the roof anchor it to the icy ground. Take only two steps from the cooking stove and the temperature at floor level is below freezing. Sometimes during gales the floor buckles and rolls like the waves of the sea.

The hut is small and cramped. Every surface is layered in black, sooty dust and rancid-smelling grease. Beds, table, chairs and shelves are all made out of packing cases. But it's home to fifteen men crammed together through the long dark days of winter when the sun never rises.

Shackleton's hut is exactly where he promised Scott not to be. Shackleton always intended to set up his base camp on the great ice plain of the Barrier. But when he reached the Bay of Whales, his chosen landing place, he discovered that long stretches of ice cliff had broken away, forming massive icebergs. If the Barrier really was a vast shelf of ice floating on the sea, as people were beginning to think, Shackleton feared that the edge could break off again and float away with his hut. He couldn't risk it. In the end, running out of summer weather, he had to rush stores and equipment ashore on a pebbly beach at Cape Royds, Ross Island, only a day and a half's march from Scott's old *Discovery* base at Hut Point.

So Shackleton's route to the Pole will be the same as Scott's, and familiar. But he'll have to get across some dangerous sea-ice before he can reach the Barrier's edge.

Tucked against the hut under drifts of snow are storerooms, a garage for the car, and stables. Six of his precious ponies have already died. Only four are left, Chinaman, Socks, Quan and Grisi. At the last minute, Shackleton did bring nine dogs. Puppies have been born, and they run around in the freezing cold.

Inside the hut, the men have rigged up private spaces to sleep, two in a cubicle. Personal possessions are crammed amongst vital equipment. The cubicle next to the Boss, Shackleton, is the neatest. It's got curtains, bookshelves, pictures painted on the walls, beds made cleverly out of bamboo and strips of canvas. Nicknamed 'Number 1 Park Lane', it's also the surgery and emergency operating theatre. Eric Marshall, one of the Expedition's two doctors, sleeps here. The other occupant is Jameson Adams, a merchant navy officer. They've both been chosen for the Pole journey.

The fourth member of the Pole party, Frank Wild, came south with Scott as a Royal Navy seaman. Wild and his cubicle mate Ernest Joyce sleep in the 'Rogues' Retreat', sharing the cramped space with a large sewing machine and a printing press. Shackleton wants Antarctica's first book published during the winter. Wild and Joyce had to learn how to use the printing press before they sailed from London.

Fear of the foul disease scurvy hangs over the expedition. It threatens all who spend time in the Arctic, and Antarctic, and all sailors on long sea voyages. No one knows for sure what causes it. Scurvy attacked Scott's expedition, and Marshall is determined to try and prevent it this time. He's read the latest research. He's attracted by the idea that fresh meat, lightly cooked, helps prevent scurvy. So everyone is eating plenty of seal-meat, as well as tinned fruit and tinned tomatoes. Marshall monitors the men's health tenaciously. If anyone falls sick or is injured on the Pole journey, all lives are at risk.

Shackleton and his men are cut off from all help, all contact with the outside world. Their weather-beaten ship *Nimrod* left Antarctica in February as the short summer closed in and ice began forming on the sea. Just before winter, a party scrambled to the top of Mount Erebus and stared down into its steaming crater.

Now, in the constant dark of winter and the bitter cold, men go for walks, look after the ponies and dogs, share the household jobs, help the cook, do scientific work.

Everyone is waiting for the sun to return, with its glorious light and promise of warmth. Then the sledging trips can begin.

Chapter 7

NOW OR NEVER

THE 29th of October 1908. Six years ago, Shackleton set off towards the Pole with Scott and Wilson. Now he is leading his own party. He is determined. They will get all the way.

In a trial trip over the sea-ice, the motor car travelled for nine hours, carrying a heavy weight of provisions. Six men would have taken two or three days to shift the same load the same distance, Shackleton noted gleefully. But now the motor car manages only a short distance before the wheels churn hopelessly in snowdrifts, and it is abandoned. The idea is good. But the technology isn't up to it.

The four ponies pull a sledge each. Their hooves

sink deep into the snowy surface. Sometimes they flounder up to their bellies. They sweat, and the sweat dries in cakes of ice. They need constant attention. They chew through their halters, they kick and misbehave. Their fodder is bulky. They have to drink, which means carrying extra fuel to melt snow for water. The dogs stay behind at the hut. Shackleton isn't using them.

A month ago, Shackleton hauled some food and fuel out on to the Barrier and left them at a depot. Now he plans to leave more depots along the route – vital supplies for the return journey. The ponies will be killed as they tire, to provide meat to eat. Then the four men will pull the full weight of their sledges themselves, harnessed up, British fashion.

Even if everything goes smoothly, the depots have barely enough supplies to get the men from one to the next on the way back home. There's nothing to spare, no margin for safety. The reason is simple: they can't carry the weight. The failure of the motor car and the death of more than half the ponies means that Shackleton has food for only ninety-one days.

The mountains begin to show on the right, sharp rocky peaks, grimly majestic, daunting in the clear Antarctic light. On 26 November they reach the place where Shackleton turned back with Scott and Wilson, on the last day of 1902. This is a joyful moment: real triumph. They've taken just over half the amount of time to get here, along the same route. Now, as Adams says, they are putting their feet where nobody has ever put their feet before.

Ahead, the mountain range begins veering across their route. Shackleton has been hoping that they can walk straight on across the level surface of the great ice plain all the way to the Pole. But now they will have to find a way through the mountains.

None of the four has any training in mountaineering. They don't have crampons. Only one pony, Socks, is left. They discover a massive glacier, a vast stream of ice that seems to lead up through the mountains towards the south, like a highway. They start to climb its dangerous surface, heaved into giant contortions, creased with hidden crevasses. Socks gamely pulls his sledge, plunging and sliding. But on the third day the lid of a crevasse breaks under the pony's weight and he falls with no warning into the black depths below. All that meat gone. It's a disaster.

Shackleton constantly calculates the amount of food they have left, against the distance still to go. They must keep the pace up. They are managing to travel further each day than he did with Scott and Wilson. But it's still not fast enough for their supplies to last them all the long way to the Pole, and back.

The daily ration of food has already been reduced. Now Shackleton reduces it again. They never had enough to eat in any case. They begin to suffer real hunger, their appetites sharpened by the cold, and the hard physical labour of hauling the heavy sledges.

And still they climb, slipping, dragging their sledges up the sharp ice, taking the appalling strain on their chafed shoulders, their hurting stomachs. Gritting, determined, in constant danger from hidden crevasses, toiling up the glacier that Shackleton later names the Beardmore, after the Scottish businessman who helped fund the expedition. Higher and higher, gasping for breath in the thinning air. They fall into crevasses, and dangle, saved by their ropes. They slide and tumble, their bodies cut and bruised by the sharp ice. Snow blindness attacks, and they cannot see. Burnt by the sun, their eyes feel filled with sharp, agonising grit, and ooze and leak.

At last they reach the head of the glacier. At least, they fervently hope they have. Ahead seems to be a vast ocean of ice, held back by the mountains. A high polar plateau.

Shackleton makes a decision. They will dash for the Pole. The weight of their loaded sledges is slowing them down. Surely travel will be easier up on the level plateau? They dump a pile of equipment under high rocks, leaving behind everything but the barest necessities. Even their spare clothing. Now they only have what they stand up in. It's thin and wearing out, but they'll have to manage. The weather is staying wonderfully fine.

There's a bit more than 300 miles to go to the Pole. They feel very hopeful. Travelling light like this, they reckon they'll do it in three weeks. They are behind the timetable they've set themselves. But by cutting down on food, they can stretch their supplies to last 120 days.

That leaves no margin at all.

What Shackleton doesn't reckon on, is the cold. And the awful fact that they keep on going up. Every dreadful frozen ridge, every ice-fall, every crevasse, is followed by another. And another. The head of the glacier keeps disappearing somewhere ahead. The wind is driving from the south now, straight at their weather-scarred, frost-damaged faces. It's constant, appalling, bone-chilling. They shake in their thin, worn clothes. Marshall takes their temperatures. They are dropping dangerously below normal. He checks their health. At least they show no signs of scurvy. But Shackleton suffers terrible headaches in the high altitude.

Hunger is perhaps the worst of all to bear. More than the exhaustion, the cold, the weakness, and the nightmare dragging of the sledge. They cannot stop thinking about food. Each meagre meal seems only to sharpen their terrible gnawing need to eat. Willpower, ambition, drive them on. But they are being defeated by that stubborn problem, which Shackleton struggled with, and Scott before him: how to carry enough to eat, far enough to get to the Pole. And home again.

On Christmas Day they huddle forlornly in their tent, surrounded by drifting snow and dreary frozen wastes. They eat some carefully hoarded, long-anticipated treats. A week ago they began their dash. They hold a council of war and decide to dump more gear, and reduce their food ration. Again.

It's 'now or never', Marshall writes in his diary.

Chapter 8

WE HAVE DONE OUR BEST

9 January 1909. The night in the tent has been unrelentingly miserable. Four men squashed in a space meant for two. Thin worn-out tent walls strumming, the wind outside shrieking. Drift-snow powdering their damp, half-frozen sleeping bags. Troubled shivering sleep, feet hovering on the edge of fatal frostbite. Dreaming as always of food. But however the food appears – flying jam tarts, big juicy roast beef, pies stuffed with meat – they never manage to eat their dream meals. Waking, weak, famished, to damp socks pulled over cracked swollen feet, to a shrivelled, aching stomach, to one cup of thin cocoa and half a biscuit.

For sixty hours a blizzard has roared, trapping them in the tent like insects helpless in a huge, alien landscape. Now at last the wind is dropping.

The end has come. They've known for some days that they can't make it. The disappointment is terrible. All that's left is one final rush. Leave everything behind, get as close as they can. Shackleton wants to get within a hundred miles of the Pole. That will help ease the misery of failure.

At 4.00 a.m. the four men leave the little tent and the sledge. Taking just biscuits and a bit of chocolate in their pockets, free now from the dragging weight around their stomachs, they half-run, half-walk across the white surface, the relentless, endless surface of snow and ice, south, towards that tiny spot on the globe called the South Pole.

After five hours they stop. Marshall, who is navigating, calculates their position as 88 degrees 23 minutes south. Using explorers' measurements, the same as sailors use, he says they are ninety-seven nautical miles, or 112 statute miles, short of the Pole.

They raise their flags, one the gift of Queen Alexandra, carried all this long way. Shackleton takes possession of the country for King Edward VII.

Peering south, they see nothing but the desolate white snow plateau. They snatch a couple of photographs, then Shackleton orders the retreat.

They head back to their tent, load the sledge, harness themselves up, and begin retracing their footsteps, clearly marked in the snow. Homeward bound at last.

Chapter 9

THE POLE ISN'T WORTH A LIFE

A new, deadly race has begun. The race for survival.

Shackleton has taken enormous risks. He has left few depots, and the distances between them are very long. Each depot is marked in the vast white emptiness by a heap of snow and a single flag. They will have to rely on their footprints and sledge tracks to guide them back. But blizzards could wipe out all their tracks. Or bad weather could delay them, trapping them in their tent.

At least the endless wind is behind them now. They hoist a sail using the tent floor-cloth, and speed along, the sledge lurching, but making fast time. In eleven days they have reached the depot near the top of the glacier where they left their spare clothing. The next depot is over a hundred miles down at the bottom of the glacier. Climbing up took two weeks. Now they have just five days' food.

They hurtle down the glacier, miraculously avoiding hidden crevasses. Lose their way. Finish all their food. Keep going only on special cocaine pills brought by Marshall for this kind of emergency. Shackleton is very ill. Wild collapses, then Adams. Marshall manages to struggle alone to the depot in a desperate attempt to fetch food, breaking through the lids of three crevasses on the way. But he makes it. They are down from the crippling high altitude and terrible cold. They are back on the great ice plain.

It's 28 January. The short summer is beginning to finish. Now they are racing against the changing season. A storm beats in, confining them to their tents for two days. It's a disaster. They haven't the food to spare. Dysentery attacks each of them, reducing their strength. They think that the frozen horsemeat is to blame. But at least there is still no scurvy.

Three small depots lie strung out across the empty

white plain. Each has to be found, with no delay. To their great relief, their outward tracks are still clearly visible, footprints turned into ice prints in the surface snow.

But disaster hovers always close. They are intensely, fiercely hungry. All the time. The strain is appalling. They are weak with dysentery. Each depot is reached – just. They are hanging on with grim determination, four scarecrows driving themselves forward, hauling a sledge across the white expanse. No heroics. Surviving by will power.

New worries fill their minds. Before they set out, Shackleton left orders for food to be brought out to a special depot, a few days' journey from their base hut. If no one has done it, that will be the end. They have no food left.

Worse – their ship *Nimrod* was due to arrive at their hut, collect everyone and depart for England on the last day of February. Shackleton had calculated they would be returned from the Pole a month ago. Will the ship be waiting for them? Will anyone believe that they are still alive, still desperately trying to make it back?

They reach the all-important depot, and the food is there. Almost beyond relief, they eat ravenously.

For the first time for over three months they have enough in their bellies.

They hurry on. Marshall collapses with diarrhoea, keeps going, but by 27 February he cannot move. Adams stays to look after him, and Shackleton and Wild set off for one last push.

They stumble and struggle with almost no rest for forty hours until they reach the longed-for goal – Scott's old *Discovery* hut. It's the last day of February. They have been away for 126 days.

No one is there. The hut is empty. Boarded up. Cold. They are in despair.

The Captain of *Nimrod* has given the four explorers up for dead. He brings the ship in, to land a small party of men who will stay behind for the winter and search for the bodies. Suddenly, someone on board sees a signal light flashing from Scott's hut.

'Did you get to the Pole?' a sailor calls to Shackleton, from the rigging. Failure jerks in the cold air. 1,500 gruelling miles travelled. But no Pole. To have been there on the silent, awful plateau, so close to success; to have given up, knowing when to turn back. That had taken real courage.

Shackleton leads a rescue party to find Adams and

Marshall. By 4 March everyone is on board *Nimrod* and heading north, escaping from the gathering ice of winter.

'The Pole isn't worth a life,' Shackleton had said, before he started.

Chapter 10

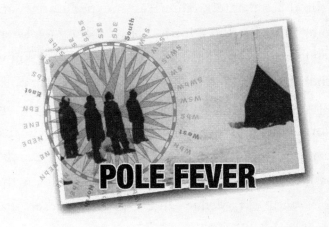

POLE FEVER

SHACKLETON returns to England a hero. The King makes him Sir Ernest. He didn't quite get to the Pole. But his attempt is a glorious near miss. To the public, Shackleton and his men battled against the odds, raced against disaster, and survived. They showed true British grit. It's a wonderful adventure with a happy ending.

And Shackleton has shown the way. The South Pole seems to lie high on an ice cap, in the middle of Antarctica.

Pole fever grips. Americans, Germans and Japanese all announce plans to get to the South Pole. There are grand ideas for expeditions to 'cross the Antarctic continent'.

Two separate American expeditions are competing for the North Pole. At least explorers struggling across the ice floes of the Arctic Sea know where they will find their goal. The Norwegian polar explorer Roald Amundsen also wants to get the North Pole. His expedition will spend four to five years drifting across the Arctic, studying the polar seas. As soon as he is in range, he will dash for the Pole with ski, sledge and dogs. Amundsen has persuaded Fridtjof Nansen to let him use his famous polar ship *Fram* for the journey.

And, of course, Scott plans to go back to Antarctica. He announces his new expedition only three months after Shackleton gets home. The South Pole must be bagged by an Englishman. Shackleton almost did it. He, Scott, will clinch it.

Scott is now a Royal Navy Captain. His expedition will carry out the usual scientific work and geographical exploration – polar expeditions need to do this to help raise funds. But central to his plans is the South Pole.

Scott studies Shackleton's attempt to achieve the Pole. Shackleton nearly did it using just four ponies. Scott will succeed by using more and better resources. He will take lots of ponies and avoid Shackleton's mistakes – keep the ponies alive on the long sea voyage from England and manage them better out on the great ice plain. Then he will use them as food, like Shackleton, because of course ponies can't get up the great glacier. Scott still does not trust dogs but he will take them. He's heard about an Englishman called Cecil Meares who knows how to drive dogs. He'll send Meares to Siberia to buy thirty-three. He'll get him to buy the ponies as well, though Meares doesn't know anything about horses. Most importantly, Scott will use the latest technology. Shackleton's motor car failed. Well, he will take something better – motorised sledges.

Scott travels to a frozen lake in Norway to watch a prototype motor sledge being tested. Petrol engine clattering and spluttering, the sledge chugs over the smooth, icy surface at four-and-a-half miles an hour, pulling three tons of weight. Scott does enthusiastic sums. At this rate it will take only fifty-five hours to get across the Barrier to the mountains. The motor sledge will be the key to the Pole.

Fridtjof Nansen tries to persuade Scott to rethink his transport. You must take skis, says Nansen. Petrol engines are still very new, and untried. But it's no good having skis unless you know how to use them properly. You ought to let a Norwegian show you how, Nansen says. And, to clinch the argument: Shackleton would have reached the Pole if he'd had skis.

Scott has never seen a really accomplished skier. Now he watches a twenty-year-old Norwegian, Tryggve Gran. Instantly, Scott is converted. Skis are the extra kind of transport he needs. They will be his insurance policy in case the motor sledges fail. He asks Gran to come with him and teach his men. Gran agrees, although he'd been planning his own expedition to Antarctica. But he is worried: how can the English learn to ski well enough in only a few months?

Scott chooses a large party to come with him. Several were on the *Discovery*, including Dr Edward Wilson, his friend, whom he trusts. The cavalry officer Lawrence Oates, and the young Oxford history graduate Apsley Cherry-Garrard, have each given very large donations to the Expedition. Scott asks Frank Wild to come and get the Pole this time. Wild refuses. He's a Shackleton man. Few of Scott's party have cold weather experience.

Like Shackleton, Scott is short of funds. School children raise money to pay for a dog, or a pony. The meteorologist's instruments are bought with funds raised in his home town.

Scott and Shackleton are similar in another important way. Not enough time is spent organising the new expedition.

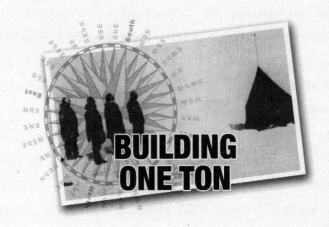

Chapter 11

BUILDING ONE TON

THE British Antarctic Expedition sails from London in a converted whaling ship, the *Terra Nova*, on the first day of June 1910. Huge crowds yell, sirens, whistles and explosions reverberate around the docks. Bagging the Pole is easy for the public to understand. They want the glory, they want Scott to get it for Britain.

Scott has decided to land at his old base, Hut Point, on Ross Island. He will cross the Barrier along the route he pioneered eight years ago, then head for the Pole up through the mountains via the Beardmore Glacier discovered by Shackleton.

Terra Nova works painfully through the ice-covered Ross Sea. To his annoyance, Scott finds sea-ice blocking his route to Hut Point. He has to land somewhere different, and chooses a beach at Cape Evans. At least his new base is a bit closer to the Barrier than Shackelton's hut at Cape Royds. But frozen sea now lies between him and the start of the route south. It's an unpredictable surface. The sea-ice could break up and drift away any time from now on.

Early in January 1911, men begin unloading crates of stores, nineteen exhausted ponies, thirty-three edgy dogs, three heavy motor sledges, from *Terra Nova*. Scott decides that supplies must be got south immediately, before winter prevents all travelling. A big depot of food and fuel needs to be created, ready for the Pole journey next summer. Young expedition members – inexperienced but enthusiastic – race around in the snow. Organising the depot trip is very rushed. Boxes of provisions are unpacked in a hurry, rations weighed out, clothes found. The supplies are ferried across the sea-ice and up on to the Barrier by a party of twelve men, eight ponies and twenty-four dogs.

Captain Oates has joined the expedition to look after the ponies. He doesn't approve of the choice –

they're broken-down old crocks, he claims. Now Scott sees for himself how ponies manage on Antarctica's ice and snow. Their hooves break through the surface, they wallow sometimes up to their bellies, they suffer. Tryggve Gran miserably discovers that it isn't possible to lead a pony while wearing skis. The ponies start failing, from cold and exposure, and from hunger. But the two dog teams scamper along enthusiastically pulling their loaded sledges.

Scott aims to set up his depot at 80 degrees south – it's a clear, significant goal. The South Pole is at 90 degrees south. Each degree of latitude is sixty nautical miles. Getting to the South Pole is like a count down – so many miles closer than anyone else, so many miles still to go.

But after twenty-four days of struggle Scott realises that conditions are too harsh to take the ponies on further. On 17 February he orders a halt thirty-two miles short of 80 degrees south. One Ton Depot is built. The cairn of snow covering about a ton of food and fuel is marked by a single black flag.

On the way back, the sea-ice breaks up and men are stranded. They camp in Scott's old *Discovery* hut at Hut Point. It's almost winter, May 13, before every man and animal has returned to Cape Evans from the depot journeys. Seven out of the eight ponies are dead; another pony has died at the hut. That leaves just ten for the attempt on the Pole, next summer. Disastrously, one of the three precious motor sledges fell through the ice while being unloaded off the ship and is lying at the bottom of the sea.

Scott's transport plans are badly dented. Worst of all, he's had terrible, unexpected news. It concerns that beak-nosed, hooded-eyed, experienced polar explorer, Roald Amundsen.

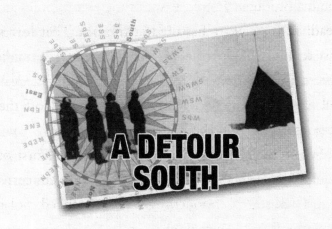

Chapter 12

A DETOUR SOUTH

R OALD Amundsen experienced the harshness of Antarctica before Scott or Shackleton ever thought of going there. Amundsen dreamed of being a polar explorer from the age of fifteen. He built up his fitness, practised mountain and cross-country skiing, then sailed north to the Arctic ice, training to be a ship's officer. Aged twenty-five, Amundsen offered to serve without pay as second mate on a private Belgian expedition to the Antarctic Peninsular. Early in winter 1898, their ship *Belgica* was trapped in the pack-ice, and did not break free for thirteen dreadful months. The men cramped below deck in the dark and bitter cold were the first humans to spend a winter in Antarctica. Some went mad, all suffered from scurvy.

The ship's doctor was an American, Frederick Cook. He'd explored in Greenland, and he taught the eager Amundsen techniques for polar travel. Amundsen learnt all he could from Cook. While the ship drifted, helplessly trapped, the two men discussed the subjects close to their hearts: exploring, equipment, expedition food. Together they designed a new tent.

Amundsen believed that polar exploring was about careful and detailed preparation, and proper equipment – about being professional. Back in Norway he carried on learning, then led a successful expedition to the Arctic.

In September 1909, Amundsen's plans for his new Arctic expedition in the *Fram* were nearly complete when amazing news broke. The North Pole had been reached. At last. Not once, but twice, and both times by Americans. Amundsen's old friend Dr Frederick Cook claimed to have got there. So did Robert Edwin Peary, who had tried many times before.

The news was a deathblow to Amundsen's hopes. The great prize of the North Pole had been won.

Amundsen couldn't see the point of going to a place where someone else had been. At the same time he needed to raise more funds for his Arctic Expedition, and now money dried up.

Publicly, Amundsen announced that he would still spend four to five years drifting in *Fram* in the ice of the Arctic Sea, doing scientific and oceanographic research. He would not change his plans.

Privately, Amundsen acted fast. One Pole was taken. He would get the remaining one. On the long way round South America to Alaska to begin his expedition, he would stop off and conquer the South Pole. That would be the spectacular achievement he needed. It would make his name as an explorer. The publicity would pay for his Arctic expedition.

Scott announced his new Antarctic expedition, never dreaming that he had a rival. Amundsen worried about the secrecy – he didn't want Scott to think he was sneaking south just to get ahead of him. But the people who had already put money into his expedition might stop him if they knew about this change to his plans. Amundsen decided that he had to make all his preparations without telling anyone, except a few friends and family.

Amundsen sailed quietly from Norway in *Fram* at

the end of June 1910, almost a month after Scott's ship left London. His carefully chosen men were very surprised when ninety-seven noisy Greenland dogs were hoisted aboard. Why did they need these new shipmates? And why was there a heavy prefabricated hut strapped to the deck with a kitchen table, and a cooker? Who needed that in the floating ice of the Arctic?

At the tropical island of Madeira, their first stop, Amundsen unrolled a map of Antarctica and announced the addition to the expedition's plans. His men listened, mouths dropping open in astonishment. It won't take long, said Amundsen. It's just a detour on the way to the Arctic. No scientific work will be done. That will come later, in the Arctic. The only reason for going south is to win the Pole. It's a question of racing the English.

'Hurrah!' shouted the champion skier Olav Bjaaland. 'That means we'll get there first!'

Amundsen had already decided to set up his base camp on the Barrier. He believed that choosing the right starting point for the Pole journey was half the battle. Here on the great ice plain, the road south would stretch from his front door.

But he didn't want Scott to find out where he

planned to land. He knew that Scott intended returning to his old base on Ross Island and starting from there. Good.

Fram arrived at the ice edge at the Bay of Whales in the middle of January 1911. Here, the ice cliff was low enough to land the stores. When Shackleton tried to land here he decided that he could not trust the ice. But Amundsen was convinced that the ice was safe enough to build his hut. In February, *Fram* sailed for Buenos Aires to do oceanographic research, leaving behind a small team of nine men to face the winter, and get to the Pole.

While he was in Australia, on his way south, Scott received a cable from Amundsen with the extraordinary information that he was heading for Antarctica. Scott tried to ignore the news. He had no idea where Amundsen would land. He hoped it would be way over on the other side.

Then, early in February 1911, some of Scott's men exploring in *Terra Nova* along the edge of the Barrier came across *Fram*, and met the Norwegians.

So now Scott knows exactly where Amundsen is. Sixty miles closer to the Pole than him. A whole degree of latitude. The *Terra Nova* officers reported that Amundsen had top skiers and fast-moving dog teams – the Norwegians enjoyed giving them a demonstration. The Norwegians, said the officers, were obviously used to hardship, well organised, good-humoured: they were very dangerous rivals.

And now Scott knows he is in a race. Not a race where one man tries, then stands aside for the next. This time the contestants will compete together.

Scott broods. There's no doubt that Amundsen's plan is a very serious menace to theirs. He fears that – unless Amundsen has bad luck – he will get to the Pole first. So he decides again to ignore the subject. The British Antarctic Expedition will carry on as if Amundsen had never appeared. Go forward, do their best for the honour of country without, says Scott, 'fear or panic'.

Chapter 13

WINTER IN FRAMHEIM

THE Norwegians call their hut Framheim. It's small, but they solve the space problem by tunnelling down into the ice and digging out caves to use as workshops, connected by passages. They even build a laundry, a sauna and a lavatory.

Before winter begins, Amundsen and his men set up a large depot of food and fuel on the great ice plain at 80 degrees south. They expected travelling to be hard for dogs, hard for sledges. Scott and Shackleton had described the Barrier in such harsh terms. But the teams of dogs pull the sledges efficiently and fast. The Norwegians decide that the dreaded Barrier is not very different from travelling over a glacier at home, after all.

So Amundsen decides to go further along the route to the Pole and make two more depots, at 81 degrees and 82 degrees south. But these next trips are very tough. Temperatures fall far below zero and eleven dogs die, worn out in the harsh cold. At least the men now have more than enough supplies in three large depots, stretching 200 miles towards the Pole. Amundsen marks the depots clearly, and flags the route to them carefully. He isn't interested in risk-taking on the Pole journey. He wants real margins of safety.

Amundsen is equally obsessed with equipment. The sledges didn't run well on the depot journeys, so the carpenter rebuilds them. Saving weight is vital and he makes them as light as possible. Amundsen has designed a wooden case to fit on the sledges, with a round opening in the top, closed with an aluminium lid. Aluminium is a new material, lightweight and rustproof. Now instead of having to unstrap a case to open it, a man just needs to pull off the round aluminium lid and reach inside. At the end of each long day's sledging on the Pole journey, every task will be tiring for weary men in the bitter cold, so every job saved is worthwhile.

For the same reason, sledging rations are reduced down to just four ingredients: chocolate, dried milk, biscuits and pemmican – ground-up dried meat mixed with lard. Amundsen has added dried vegetables and oatmeal to his pemmican, and also has a version for the dogs that humans can eat if they have to. The sledging rations are weighed out and packed with care so each day's allowance can be easily reached.

Each man works on his own ski boots to make them bigger. Feet must be able to move inside boots to prevent freezing. In a snow cave, one of the men sits at a sewing machine, remaking the tents that weren't satisfactory on the depot journeys. The tents are white. Then someone thinks of dying them with ink, to be visible against the snow, to absorb warmth, and rest eyes in the dazzling light of the Antarctic summer.

The winter passes quickly. There's so much work to do. Each man has useful skills. Many are experienced polar travellers. Every decision and action relates to the one aim of victory. They live simply, all together, Amundsen insisting on seal-meat for lunch and dinner because experience shows it helps prevent scurvy.

During his expedition to the Arctic, Amundsen met the Netsilik people living on the far northern shores of Canada. He learnt from them how to build igloos, and watched how they harnessed their strong dogs to sledges. They taught him the difficult art of dog-driving. He traded for their clothes, and learnt the right way to wear them. The Netsiliks wore fur anoraks – large, long, loose jackets with attached hoods, designed to protect the face against cold and wind. They wore loose fur trousers. Their clothes allowed the warmth from their bodies to be easily trapped. At the same time, air could circulate, preventing sweating. Sweat is dangerous in the cold, dragging heat away from the body, wetting clothing. The sweat freezes in the frigid air and melts again when warmed, in a cycle of misery for the wearer.

Amundsen has ordered clothing for the South Pole trip made on the Netsilik pattern. There are anoraks and trousers in four different materials: wolf skin, reindeer fur, English Burberry windproof cloth, Norwegian cotton gabardine. There are even sets of clothes in old military blanket material, to wear around the base.

Many other polar explorers understand how much can be learnt from the people who live in the

Arctic – those experts in the art of surviving in deep cold. But Amundsen is unusual in tracking down exactly what he wants. His sleeping bags, for example, have an outer bag of heavy buck reindeer-skin, and an inner bag of thin female reindeer-skin. Amundsen needed all his contacts to get the right fur, and now he has it.

But beyond everything else, it's the sledge dogs that matter. The thieving, fighting, rowdy, bullying, brave, intelligent, loyal Eskimo dogs. They are the engines of the expedition. Without them, the Pole is impossible for Amundsen. The men's lives will depend on them. The dogs live in big tents sunk in the snow, chained up at night and free to roam in the day. Each man looks after fourteen or fifteen. On silent winter nights, when the moon shines over the enormous ice plain, the dogs howl, in long, lonely howls.

These are not domesticated pet dogs. They will fight to the death. They have to be understood, and properly managed. They have to give their trust. They have to know who is master. They have their own hierarchy, and the lead dog is king. Amundsen is a competent dog driver but he's got two top dog drivers with him. The biggest threat Amundsen has over his men is the fear of what he calls that 'futile toil', of being harnessed to sledges and having to pull. The Norwegians see the man-hauling harness as a symbol of failure to succeed with dogs.

All winter Amundsen worries about Scott. What is he doing? What is he planning? When will he start? Will those motor sledges succeed? Scott knows the route. Amundsen must pioneer a new one across the Barrier. He must find a new way up through the mountains. The whole thing is meaningless unless they achieve the Pole. That's the only reason they are here. Amundsen plans and re-plans, uneasy, restless.

Amundsen orders the expedition to be ready to depart the day the first glimpse of sun appears after the long months of darkness, on 24 August. He'll take everyone except the cook. He can't risk waiting.

But the cold is impossible and they cannot leave. Amundsen fidgets, and worries. Surely spring is on its way. At last, on 8 September, they set off, dogs galloping ahead with the sledges.

It's too early. Men and dogs suffer and struggle in the deep cold. Amundsen has to order a retreat. The Chief, as his men call him, has made a bad mistake. His ability as a leader is questioned by Hjalmar

Johansen, the most experienced polar explorer amongst his men, and he and Amundsen have an unforgiving row. Four men have badly frostbitten heels and can't leave their bunks. Some of the dogs die, the others rest their blood-caked, frostbitten paws. At least the time can be used to adjust the equipment again. The boots are still too stiff.

Amundsen has to wait until it gets a bit warmer. Unhappy, tense, tormented with thoughts of defeat.

Picture 1 (above): Shackleton's party starting for the Pole from the edge of the Barrier. Three of the loaded sledges can be seen, and (left to right) the ponies Socks, Grisi and Quan.

Picture 2 (insert): Ernest Shackleton as a young man in London before he went to the Pole.

Picture 3 (right): Roald Amundsen on board *Fram* in Oslo, with his Antarctic plans still a secret.

Picture 4 (below): A campsite on Amundsen's South Pole expedition. The dogs rest while the men take observations to check their position. You can see the bicycle wheel that was part of a sledgemeter, used to log the distance covered.

Picture 5 (right): Robert Scott working in his room in the hut at Cape Evans, winter 1911.

Picture 6 (below): The South Pole. Scott and his men, with their flags. Standing, left to right: Titus Oates, Robert Scott, 'Taff' Evans. Sitting, left to right: 'Birdie' Bowers, Edward Wilson.

Picture 7 (top): The Norwegians at the South Pole, with the tent they left there.

Picture 8 (below): Oscar Wisting with his dog team at the South Pole, December 1911.

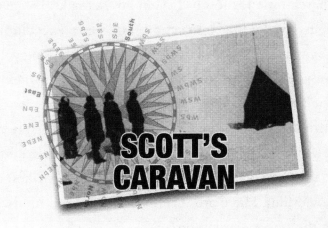

Chapter 14

SCOTT'S CARAVAN

I N the hut at Cape Evans, a wall of packing cases with a narrow opening divides the interior. Sixteen officers and scientists live on one side. On the other are the Royal Navy men who aren't officers, plus the cook, a steward to serve at table, and two Russians who speak very little English – a groom and a dog-driver. Scott naturally runs the expedition in naval style, and feels everyone is more comfortable knowing their familiar place. His men call him 'the Owner'.

Everyone gets on well, but there are tensions. The presence of Amundsen, established on the Barrier, casts a real shadow.

Every day the scientists manage to do some work. There's time for football. Men go on walks. Tryggve Gran gives skiing instruction, but some expedition members are irritated that skiing isn't something you can just 'do'. The ponies need a lot of looking after. The two remaining motor sledges don't work particularly well. Lectures are given. An expedition newspaper is written. Wilson the doctor paints watercolours. Ponting the photographer makes a movie film. There are various accidents and injuries on the unfamiliar icy surface.

In the coldest middle of winter, when the sun never rises, three of the men picked for the southern journey go on a gruelling expedition to collect some Emperor penguin eggs. Dr Edward Wilson, Henry 'Birdie' Bowers, a tough strong sub-lieutenant in the Royal Indian Marines, and twenty-five-year-old Apsley Cherry-Garrard, desperately short-sighted, who has been brought south as assistant zoologist. They suffer dreadfully and nearly die. Scott christens their journey 'the worst journey in the world'.

Scott has a restlessly enquiring mind, but he is impatient and can fail to listen to advice. Now he has real worries. He makes plans for the journeys to come, then changes them. There will be various short trips in spring to train men in polar travelling, and to build up supplies. A summer expedition will be undertaken to the Western Mountains. The endless problem, the real headache, is transport for the Pole journey. Scott juggles the options, hoping the motor sledges will do well, then losing faith in them; wondering whether ponies can make it up the glacier after all; deciding how far he can trust the dogs. 'I see the difficulty of complicated transport,' Gran had written in his diary after the trip setting up One Ton Depot. 'We will need luck if we are to reach the Pole.'

By midwinter, preparations have begun for the summer journeys ahead. Everyone is eager, willing. Sledge rations are weighed and packed, clothing altered, reindeer-fur sleeping bags sewn. The men have special woollen Jaeger underwear, and fur boots called finnesko as used by the Lapps. The British version of the Arctic anorak is made out of Burberry cloth. The clothes are hardwearing and windproof. But they trap sweat from hard-working bodies. The sweat freezes then melts, resulting in dangerously damp clothes. The jacket has no hood. Men wear a variety of wool-lined helmets and hats, but vital warmth escapes from around their necks.

Scott cannot make an early start, because the ponies are unable to stand too much cold. So his caravan begins winding out from the hut late in October. Just before he departs south, Scott writes to his agent in New Zealand. Of course Amundsen's presence has complicated the situation, Scott says. But any attempt at a race could have been fatal to the British chance of getting to the Pole. So he decided to do exactly as he would have done had Amundsen not been down here. 'If he gets to the Pole,' writes Scott, 'he is bound to do it rapidly with dogs . . . If he fails, he ought to hide! . . . But he is not there yet!'

Scott's final plan of attack on the Pole uses all available types of transport. First to leave are the two motor-sledges, grinding forward for as long as they can. Then come the two slowest ponies, James Pigg and Jehu. On the first day of November the main party leaves with the rest of the ponies, setting out in three stages, according to their speed. The dog teams trot back and forth along the line, carrying equipment. Travelling is unavoidably complicated with each type of transport moving at a different speed.

Out across the great ice plain, Scott's party straggles. The motor sledges soon fail, and are abandoned. The ponies struggle through the snow, sinking at each step. At the end of every day they must be rubbed down, fed, and snow walls built to protect them from the wind. The suffering ponies find it difficult to cope. Scott 'carries a face like a tired seaboot', writes Captain Oates. But, to Scott's surprise, the dog teams race past easily. Scott hadn't planned to take the dogs far, and there isn't enough food for them. Now he uses the dogs to ferry fodder to the ponies, but the weakest pony has to be killed to feed the hungry dogs.

The goad Scott uses to drive himself on is not Amundsen, but the unseen presence of Shackleton. Shackleton is the rival he pits himself against. His timings, his daily distances, the weather he experienced. Shackleton almost made it to the Pole with less equipment and resources. It must just be a question of pushing harder, going the extra distance.

Shackleton started with four ponies. He, Scott, starts with ten ponies. Shackleton didn't use dogs, but Scott does. Shackleton didn't use skis. Scott is. Shackleton travelled with only three companions, but Scott has fifteen men in a complex pattern of support parties. The numbers will gradually drop away, until in the end he'll have a team of four, tried and tested, aiming for the heart of the Pole, like the head of a spear. He must be able to do it.

There is a schedule that must be kept to. So many miles achieved each day. So much food and fuel used, and no more. Otherwise supplies won't last. It's the old problem. Scott experienced it on his first trip south. Shackleton struggled with it. Scott already has his One Ton Depot, laid on the Barrier after they arrived in Antarctica. Now, like Shackleton, he plans to lay two more depots across the Barrier.

Every delay, every setback is unacceptable to Scott. He can't afford it, so can't allow for it. But of course the inevitable bad weather happens, and poor snow conditions, slowing the ponies and the men, gamely plodding. Blizzards blow across the ice plain and the men have to stay idle in their tents, while the ponies shiver outside. The surface changes – difficult, easier, rough, thick – like sandpaper, or sticky, or gritty, or too soft. It's confusing, unpredictable. Scott frets and suffers. It's a terrible strain on him, and his men. He writes bitterly in his diary about his bad luck.

In twenty-nine days from his personal start on 1 November, Scott reaches the point where he and Wilson turned back last time with Shackleton.

Ponies continue to be shot, as their fodder runs out. Their meat provides food for the dogs, and humans.

Then – just a day's travelling from the start of Shackleton's great glacier – a blizzard roars in. Men lie in their sleeping bags while thick snow piles high and the temperature freakishly rises to just above freezing. Clothes, sleeping bags, tents – everything is soaked.

'Miserable, utterly miserable,' writes Scott in his diary. 'A hopeless feeling descends . . . and is hard to fight off.' His planning couldn't have been improved, he writes. Every detail of equipment is right. Now, almost at the end of the first stage of their journey, they are forced into dreadful inactivity – throwing everything into risk, making him fall behind Shackleton's timing. Shackleton, he convinces himself, didn't have to put up with such appalling, unexpected weather. It's a serious blow. Undeserved.

But Scott cannot control Antarctica. The weather will do what it will, when it will. The ice and snow conditions will be what they are. He will be held up when the blizzards blow. On days when the curious white light of Antarctica happens, and sky mixes with land, and shadows don't work properly, and no man can judge where to step safely, and small ridges loom like hills, and hollows don't show – he will have to cope, by stumbling on, or waiting.

There is no malevolent fate in Antarctica. Bad luck. Good luck. Each day has to be taken as it comes. What matters is how each man reacts to these great, impersonal forces.

Trapped in his dripping tent, baling water off the floor cloth, twenty-eight-year-old Birdie Bowers confides to his diary, 'Amundsen has probably reached the Pole by now. I hope he has not, as I regard him as a sneaking, back-handed ruffian.'

After four days the blizzard eases, and they can advance a few difficult miles through soft new snow to the start of the Beardmore Glacier. At least they don't have to spend time finding a way up through the mountains. They have Shackleton's route to follow.

It's 9 December. Scott has been travelling for thirty-nine days. The five remaining exhausted ponies are shot and their bodies piled in a depot for the return journey. It's a messy business, killing ponies. Four sledges and some personal gear are left behind at this camp, called the Shambles.

The mountains rear up. The glacier stretches ahead. At the top is the high plateau. And the Pole.

Chapter 15

RUNNING THEIR OWN RACE

IT'S almost three weeks into October before Amundsen makes his second departure for the Pole. This time he takes only four companions: the champion skier Olav Bjaaland, two expert dog-drivers Sverre Hassel and Helmer Hansen, and Oscar Wisting.

They have fifty-two dogs pulling four sledges.

'The English have loudly and openly told the world that skis and dogs are unusable in these regions and that fur clothes are rubbish,' Amundsen confided to his diary, in the dark of winter. 'We will see – we will see.'

Now the test has come. The conquest of that great prize, the South Pole.

In five days the men reach their first depot at 80 degrees south. They lie around resting. There's plenty of food, even more now there's a smaller party. The dogs curl in the snow, their stomachs full of seal meat brought out in autumn by the last depot-laying party.

Over at Cape Evans the two motor sledges are just chugging away from the hut on the start of Scott's complex offensive.

But in Amundsen's mind, those worrying motor sledges could already have dragged their three tons of supplies far out over the Barrier. Amundsen is using sledges, dogs and fur clothes. It's time-honoured polar equipment, developed by the native people of the far north, honed in the Arctic. Scott has put his faith in modern technology, the future. With the latest technology perhaps he doesn't need all the carefully gathered expertise Amundsen must rely on.

The South Pole sits at 90 degrees south. Amundsen intends to go straight there, the shortest route, whatever is in the way. He plans to mark his journey by the degrees of latitude. It's easy to feel progress that way – working down the globe to that final point at the very bottom. He's calculated that each degree should take four to five days to achieve, allowing himself a day for bad weather. If all goes well, that means travelling only five or six hours each day, giving plenty of time for rest and sleep for men and dogs. Hard work, and proper rest. That's the plan.

On 26 October they set off again. Several dogs have been set loose, leaving twelve pulling each sledge. The dogs are so rested they bound ahead. The sledges are heavily laden but the dogs pull strongly.

Leaving the depot at 80 degrees south is for Amundsen the real start of the Pole journey. He's on the Barrier. The uncertainty is over. The road stretches ahead. There's no point thinking about when Scott might have started. Now they are running their own race, deciding their own timings.

They travel through 'pea-souper fog', eyes straining ahead through dreadful light, and across a big stretch of ugly, dangerously crevassed ice. Then they reach the last of their three depots, at 82 degrees south. Here Amundsen suggests a new plan. They were going to carry everything they needed all the way to the Pole and back – travel fully loaded, be sledge-sufficient whatever happens. But the loads are heavy for the dogs. Now they will lay a series of depots, one at each new degree of latitude, leaving food and fuel for the return journey. They have more than enough supplies. That will lighten the sledges.

About every hour, after three miles' travel, they build a cairn out of nine blocks of snow as high as a man, to mark the route. It's always possible to see the last cairn from the next. As an extra precaution they leave a note with compass bearings. The dogs rest while the men build. Dogs work best with frequent rests.

A few hours after leaving the depot at 82 degrees south, they pass the farthest south reached by Scott, Wilson and Shackleton, on their first attempt at the Pole.

They are travelling a new route across the Barrier. Amundsen still has a faint hope that the mountains will curve away, that they won't have to climb, that the Pole might after all lie on the level ice plain. But four days later they see the summits of high mountains to the south. Gradually the mountains appear, rising straight out of the plain, stark rocky precipices, glittering peaks, gigantic, wild, daunting. Then a new range appears on their left. The great ice plain, they have discovered, is hemmed in by massive mountains.

Morale stays high. Amundsen has been able to

build in a real margin of safety. They have the three goods depots set up in the autumn. They can travel fast with dogs and skis. Their calculations allow time for bad weather. They have more than enough food and plenty of fuel, and they *know* it. As long as they keep to their schedule. But that means that Amundsen, like Shackleton before him, has to find a route through the mountains, fast.

By 17 November they have left the Barrier. Amundsen has always planned to use his dogs to heave the heavy sledges up through the mountains on to the high plateau. Now, travelling on his direct line, he comes to a monstrous glacier. Stupendous. Awe-inspiring. The ice of the plateau above bursts through the mountains in barely contained power, forcing its way down in massive ice-falls, its surface split and contorted in jagged crevasses and vast chasms, enormous blocks of ice tossed and tumbled. This glacier is an obstacle course, abrupt and menacing. Unlike the Beardmore Glacier, rising majestically up through a hundred miles, Amundsen's glacier rises most of its height in just eight treacherous miles.

Yet Amundsen sets the dogs at it. They scrabble and slip, panting and clawing, hauling the sledges, sometimes all the dogs harnessed to two sledges for extra power. Bjaaland the champion skier clambers up ahead, route-finding. Every step depends on his knowledge and instinct. The weather stays fine, the sun glares without cease on glittering snow and ice. The views, when they snatch a look, are beyond imagining. Up, and still up, dogs gamely climbing and dragging their loads.

They make it from Barrier to plateau in four horrible days. But now Amundsen must do what he also always planned. It's miserably difficult. Twenty-four of their hard-working dogs must be shot. They can't carry enough to feed all the dogs the whole way. 'When dog eats dog,' said Amundsen, 'only the teeth are left. And when they are very hungry, even these disappear.' Now dog eats dog. And the men do too. Fresh meat, to ward against scurvy. But instead of the happy mood that should have filled the camp after their success, there is an oppressive feeling in the air.

They left Framheim a month ago. They've come 430 miles. A blizzard sweeps in, keeping them in their tent for four days. The wind whistles and howls, the air is thick with driving snow. The dogs creep together, protecting themselves as best they can.

Unable to bear waiting any longer, Amundsen sets out again in bad light and gale-force winds. Now they have eighteen dogs pulling three sledges. The going is so heavy it's like dragging through sand. They'd hoped for a clear run over the polar plateau. But the terrain is appalling. The weather is appalling. The ice of the plateau, gathered and pinched towards the mountains, is riddled with crevasses, strained and disturbed, fractured and tumbling. They are experienced skiers but this is dangerous, sinister country. Razor-sharp ridges. Gaping crevasses in front, behind, and to both sides. Polished icy surfaces. Constant gales, wind cutting their faces, skin sore and scabbed with frostbite, snow whirling, minimal visibility so they travel blind. But Amundsen drives them on.

They take risks. Risk-taking is part of being in Antarctica. But drop your guard once, stop concentrating for a minute – Antarctica is unforgiving. Dangers are everywhere. Disaster is always hovering. There's no time for mistakes. They are high on the polar plateau. Breathing is more difficult. The cold is deeper, the wind relentless. It is a tense, exhausting time.

At last the ice of the plateau evens out, the wind

drops, the snow stops whirling. On 8 December they reach the critical point – Shackleton's furthest. 88 degrees 23 minutes south. They shout and cheer, raise the Norwegian flag and take photographs. They talk about Shackleton. Norwegians have always thought his achievement superb, given his equipment, and the short time he had to prepare. 'Pluck and grit can work wonders,' says Amundsen.

They travel on a few miles, then camp. The dogs are thin, tired, ravenous. For weeks now they've been eating anything they can find – boots, ski-bindings, the leather lashings holding the sledges together. Nothing is left lying about, and every evening on halting, the sledges are buried in snow to hide the lashings.

Amundsen decides to call a rest day on 9 December and make a final depot before the Pole. Lightening the sledges will be a relief. Their faces are raw and oozing with frostbite, and the slightest wind feels like a blunt knife sawing on their skin.

They mark the depot's position carefully. Thirty black-painted planks from empty sledging cases are pushed into the snow to the east, thirty to the west, each one a hundred paces apart, with a scrap of black flag on top of each plank, making a long line across their route. Up here on the featureless plateau they cannot afford to lose their way.

The final onslaught is ahead. From now on they are the pioneers. No one has ever left footprints here. They are farther south than any human has ever been.

As long as Scott is not in front of them.

Chapter 16

TERRIBLE SLOG

O N this very day, 9 December, Scott is at the foot of the Beardmore Glacier, 280 miles behind.

Scott has always been convinced that dogs can't climb mountains. Now, in a last-minute change of plan, he keeps them to help him on to the Glacier. Just for two days. Then Meares and the Russian dog driver Gerov are ordered to take them home. The dogs have done remarkably well, everyone agrees, but they've stayed longer than intended, and there's no dog food left. They should get back quite easily, according to Scott. Meares doubts it. There are worryingly few depots, and long gaps between them.

Now, as Scott has always planned, everything will

depend on man-hauling. Three teams of four men will heave and haul the heavy sledges up the Glacier. In a way Scott's been waiting for this. No more worrying about animals. It's up to dependable human labour. Backbreaking work, terrible slog. But Shackleton did it.

Getting a sledge moving is the worst bit. It needs ten to fifteen desperate jerks on the harness to even get it started. 'I have never pulled so hard,' notes Bowers in his diary, 'or so nearly crushed my inside into my backbone.'

Scott deliberately tests himself. He's forty-three, but he's immensely strong, with undoubted courage, driving will power. He can keep up with the best of them. He tests everyone else, setting team against team as the sledges are dragged exhaustingly up and up the Glacier. No one knows who will be chosen for the final Pole party.

The weather is fine and sunny. They sweat with the effort of hauling but as soon as they stop, they shiver in their soggy clothes. Scott discovers how useful skis are in deep snow. He's annoyed that some of his men have failed to learn how to use them.

Nearly at the top, Scott makes his decision, and orders four men to return. Leaving the supplies they have toiled so far to bring, the four, deeply disappointed, work their way back down the Glacier and across the ice plain, 440 miles home. The three sparse depots on the Barrier have had to be found by Meares, Gerov and the dogs. Now the depots must also sustain four tired man-haulers.

It's Friday 22 December. The third stage of the journey is beginning. Eight men dragging two sledges. Scott forces the pace, trying to catch up time in the race inside his head with Shackleton. At the end of a day's exhausting labour, when the men suggest a stop – let's go a bit further, says Scott. And they plod on, silent, for another hour. Creeping another mile or two towards the distant goal.

For Amundsen and his companions, degrees of latitude are lines on the map, so many laps, so many finishing posts. For Scott and his men, each degree of latitude is becoming a step on an exhausting ladder, a reminder of what still lies ahead.

The team led by Lieutenant Teddy Evans, Scott's second-in-command, has been man-hauling almost since the beginning of the Barrier. They started when the motor sledges broke down. Now they are beginning to tire. The forced pace is wearing them out. Teddy Evans is a passionate Pole-seeker. He had been planning his own expedition before he joined Scott's. He and Scott are open rivals.

On New Year's Eve, Scott orders Evans' team to abandon their skis and continue on foot. Scott's team continues skiing – which is faster. After camping, the three Navy men, William Lashley, Tom Crean and 'Taff' Evans, begin dismantling the sledges. Their fingers are clumsy in the bitter cold. They breathe harshly in the high altitude. They work for eight hours, shortening the length of both sledges to reduce their weight – a plan Scott has always intended. But big burly Taff Evans cuts his hand badly.

Three days later, Scott decides he can definitely do without the 'foot party' – the final support team. He is on the plateau. The Pole is 150 miles away, a straight run. Now he can come down to what he considers the-tried-and-tested head of the arrow. And that will be his own team. Himself. His old companion Dr Edward Wilson, now aged thirty-nine. Captain Lawrence Oates, nicknamed 'Titus', aged thirty-one, representing the Army. Petty Officer Edgar Evans, nicknamed 'Taff', aged thirty-five, representing the 'lower deck' of the Navy.

Scott enters the tent of Teddy Evans and tells him his decision. His team were on their way to the Pole.

Now they are relegated, the last of the support parties. But Scott asks for one of Evans' team, strong, dependable little Birdie Bowers.

Everything has been planned for teams of four. Tents hold four. All food and fuel is measured out for a team of four. A few days ago, Scott ordered Evans' team to give up their skis, so now, much shorter than the others, Birdie Bowers will have to run to keep up. But Scott wants him for the Polar party. He reveals no reason for this major change of plan in his diary. Perhaps he thinks five men will be safer than four, or the extra power will make the difference. In any case, Bowers knows navigation and Scott needs a navigator to be sure that he actually has reached the Pole.

But there are other problems. Taff Evans' cut hand isn't healing. Titus Oates is limping. His feet are continually wet and beginning to suffer damage. His left thigh, wounded by a bullet in the Boer War, is troubling him. Scott has men in his team who are weakening.

The parting comes on 4 January 1912. Three lonely men saying farewell to five lonely men on the great silent white plateau. Teddy Evans and his companions, Petty Officers Tom Crean and William

Lashley, turn back. Tough Crean half in tears, everyone affected. They have a long dangerous journey to get home, nearly the same length as Shackleton on his Pole attempt. But three men are pulling instead of four.

Scott, Wilson, Oates, Bowers, Taff Evans, face towards the Pole. It's the final effort. They must do it. Scott sends positive letters back with Teddy Evans. 'A last note from a hopeful position. I think it's going to be all right. We have a fine party going forward and arrangements are going well.'

To his wife Scott writes '. . . no man will or can say I wasn't fit to lead through the last lap.'

Five days later Scott writes the triumphant word in his diary. 'RECORD'. He has reached Shackleton's furthest point, 88 degrees 23 minutes south. It is 9 January 1912, *exactly* three years after Shackleton, to the day.

At last. Scott has beaten his rival. From this moment on, all will be new, all theirs.

Scott is now travelling in a directly comparable way with Shackleton. The support parties have gone. He is alone with his sledge companions, man-hauling for their lives.

Chapter 17

SHALL WE SEE THE ENGLISH FLAG?

IT's 10 December 1911. Amundsen, Bjaaland, Hansen, Hassel and Wisting are finding breathing a real effort. Skiing is hard so high on the plateau. At least the weather has improved. And they know how long it will take to get to the Pole, because they are keeping to their daily distance of fifteen miles.

But will they be first? Scott haunts the conversation. They check in all directions, anxiously watching the dogs as they seem to sniff the air to the south with unexplained interest. Squinting their eyes behind their snow goggles. Looking for signs of sledge tracks, heaped up snow, markers that someone has been here.

Thursday evening, 14 December, they camp

exactly fifteen miles from the Pole. Everything is going according to plan. As long as – as long as the English are not in front of them. 'The excitement is great,' Bjaaland writes in his diary. 'Shall we see the English flag – God have mercy on us, I don't believe it.'

After breakfast on Friday they set off, looking ahead, seeing only the white expanse of snow. Dogs trotting, the swish of skis. Suddenly – 'Halt!' It's three o'clock in the afternoon, 15 December 1911. They have arrived. The same endless snow. The same silence. And no English. They have done it.

Amundsen gets the Norwegian flag, held on a pair of ski sticks lashed together the night before. He asks each of his companions to clasp it. Together they plant the flag in the snow. They'd all risked their lives in the fight, wrote Amundsen. All had stood together through thick and thin. They all deserved the right to claim the Pole.

Then they get down to work. Measurements must be taken to prove that they really have got here. Amundsen doesn't want doubts and disputes like those after the two American parties claimed the North Pole. The measurements are difficult. Finding the exact spot on the globe that is the Pole isn't easy, especially with the instruments they have. As a precaution Amundsen sends his men skiing out in various directions to 'box' the space, laying markers with black flags, and notes for Scott.

Far away in the Western Mountains, Tryggve Gran has a dream. He jumps up waking the others. His dream has been so clear he writes it down in his diary. 'I dreamt I had a telegram reading: "Amundsen reached Pole 15 December".'

At the Pole, Amundsen calculates that he has enough fuel and food to spend several days doing the measurements. It's a bit of an anticlimax after all the striving. He feels curiously blank. He'd wanted the North Pole, desperately. Instead here he is, standing on the opposite end of the world.

On Sunday 17 December they ski to what they reckon is the exact spot for the South Pole, and take more measurements. When they have finished, they pitch a tiny bluey-grey tent in the vast white emptiness, a tent modelled on the design Amundsen worked out all those years ago with Cook on board *Belgica*. They put some spare equipment inside for Scott and his men to use if they want, and a letter to King Haakon of Norway, with a letter to Scott asking him to forward it to the King. The way home is long. Their hut on the great ice shelf is 700 miles tough travelling away. Much can happen.

At half past seven in the evening of Monday 18 December Amundsen and his men put on their skis and head north. They are beginning a new race. Scott will surely soon be here, any day now. They must get back quickly. It's vital to be first with the news of their victory.

At these latitudes the summer sun is in the sky all twenty-four hours. They travel at night, because then the dazzle on the snow surface is less. Three dogs die of exhaustion – a terrible worry. They utterly depend on their dogs. But after eating their companions, the remaining dogs seem to get a bit stronger.

Nearing the mountains, they lose their way. Nothing looks familiar. For the first time, the cold begins to get into their bones. It's time they were down from the high altitudes. Gradually they get their bearings. Amundsen speeds up the rate of travel. Then they are at the top of the mighty glacier, and launching themselves over the edge, dropping down, down the fearful slopes, round the abysses, between the yawning crevasses.

At the bottom another dog collapses and dies. That leaves twelve.

Now he's reached the Barrier, Amundsen really races. His expedition has been based around speed. In a way it's been like a well-planned raid – and when you're raiding, there's safety in speed. Especially in the unpredictable Antarctic climate. Now they travel twenty miles at a time instead of fifteen – camp for only eight hours – then they're out of the sleeping bags again and on. Up on the plateau, they lost track of day and night, of the date. Just as well we know what year it is! Amundsen jokes.

The weather shifts unpleasantly – sometimes so thick they can't see the tips of their skis, sometimes harsh blizzard winds howling and beating, sometimes snow, and micro-fine ice crystals that fill the air and work into every crack and crevice. But the path of beacons and depots planned by Amundsen across the great ice plain allows them to keep travelling in poor conditions. Crucially, there is more than enough food. Their stomachs are full. The dogs are actually putting on weight. Supplies are left behind at every depot – they were safety nets, now they are not needed. But disasters and emergencies had to be planned for. All Amundsen's careful effort and thinking is paying off.

At four o'clock in the morning, Friday 26 January 1912, they slip quietly up to their hut. It's ten days before they are due back. Amundsen has planned their arrival time carefully. They undo the latch of the door. Four men are sleeping soundly in their beds. 'Good morning!' calls Amundsen. 'Have you any coffee for us?'

The surprise is wonderful. 'Have you been there?' someone asks. 'Yes, we've been there,' says Amundsen. They all sit down to pancakes and jam and delicious hot coffee. Real, deep pleasure. Ninety-nine days away. 1,400 miles safely travelled.

Fram has already arrived. They pack, clean the hut, lock the door, and are on board by 30 January. The expedition has done everything it set out to do, just as intended. While five of them conquered the Pole, three others reached the new land at the opposite end of the Barrier from Ross Island; and *Fram* has done useful oceanographic work.

Then they head for Tasmania. Racing to break the news of the conquest of the Pole to the world, first, before Scott can do it.

Chapter 18

THE WORST HAS HAPPENED

THEY'RE taking longer than Scott expected. Travelling on the high plateau is hard. Much harder than he'd thought. The surface is difficult – sharp edged furrows and ridges of ice, like waves, or deep snow like gritty sand. The cold bites their fingers through layers of gloves and fur mitts, their mouths ice up. Tugging at the creaking sledge is monotonous, miserable slog. The strain of such constant physical labour is telling. They're gnawingly hungry, always thirsty. 'It is a critical time,' Scott notes at the end of another grinding day, with forty miles still to go. 'But we ought to pull through.'

★   ★   ★

All the way from the start of the Barrier, Scott has focused on his personal rivalry with Shackleton. Now he's beaten him. He's beyond the place where Shackleton had to turn back. But sometimes, the contestant you ignored slips past. At last, Scott admits to the appalling possibility. The Norwegian flag might already be there, ahead of them, at the Pole.

What they see is a distant black speck, which turns into one of Amundsen's black marker flags tied to a sledge bearer.

That night in the tent is bad. No one sleeps much. They talk, shocked, unhappy. Wilson says Amundsen turned it into a race, and in that sense beat them. Bowers says it's good that they will achieve the Pole by the traditional British sledging method. Oates, the cavalry officer who has always hated 'wretched man-hauling', writes privately that he reckons the Norskies must have had a comfortable trip with their dog teams. For Scott, the daydreams are over. 'The worst has happened, or nearly the worst.'

Next day – a gusting mean wind in their frostbitten faces, dull thick sky, deeply chilled – they arrive at the Pole. It is Wednesday 17 January 1912. 'Great God!' writes Scott. 'This is an awful place.'

Their measurements to establish the actual

position of the Pole have to be hurried, because they have no spare food. Signs of the Norwegians are everywhere. After months of loneliness it's deeply unsettling to see tracks in the snow, reminders of dogs, finally the little bluey-grey tent, with yellow wood tent pegs, Norwegian flags flying, and inside the letter to Scott. Now Scott knows that Amundsen reached the Pole a month ago.

They establish their own position for the South Pole. Put up their flags. Pose for photographs. Then leave.

A DESPERATE STRUGGLE

8⁰⁰ miles of solid man-hauling lie ahead. Scott talks about 'the run home'. He sees it as 'a desperate struggle to get the news through first'. Their ship *Terra Nova*, due back in Antarctica to bring supplies and pick up some of the men, will be leaving again in March. It was terrible to have laboured to the Pole without the reward of being first, but that was impossible to know without going there. The South Pole is won. Amundsen's made it. He's made it. Now, telling the British story is vital.

Like Shackleton, their depots on the way back are few, with long gaps between. They will need to find the tracks left by their feet in the snow. There is not enough food and fuel spare for emergencies, for bad weather, mistakes, or accidents. The motor sledges were meant to have solved everything by moving supplies across the Barrier. But they failed. In the end Scott has only what could be carried on the sledges.

And they have further to travel than Shackleton. He stopped ninety-seven miles short of the Pole. It's taken Scott eight days to do those final miles. Each extra day spent travelling at this time of the year is risky. The short summer is closing down. Temperatures are dropping. The sun swings daily lower in the sky and already it's chillingly cold. Winter is ahead. Shackleton, three years before, turned for home on 9 January. Now, Scott is setting out for home nearly one hundred miles further south, on 18 January. And Amundsen left the Pole a whole month ago.

Tired, worn, disappointed men make poor pack-horses. However hard they try.

Scott does not admit to being worried by the lateness of the season. He does not discuss plans with his men. In any case, his plans always involved travelling in February and March.

Forcing the pace, Scott makes good time to

the top of the Beardmore Glacier. But on the descent, they lose their way. Precious time is wasted. They almost run out of food. Worryingly, Taff Evans is failing. His fingers and nose are badly frostbitten, the cut on his hand won't heal. He is deeply upset by being beaten to the Pole; he falls easily, is sluggish, depressed.

Five men crammed in a four-man tent with one losing his ability to cope, irritating and worrying the others. Illness is desperate on an expedition. The failure of one threatens all. Taff Evans did the 'fixing' work, the mending and adjusting. He's the biggest, heaviest man. Scott relied on his strength. Now he's ill, slow, only able to stumble doggedly along in his traces, trying to pull. He can't manage; is left behind to catch up; fails, falls, loses consciousness. Evans dies in the tent on the night of 17 February, aged thirty-five. The four remaining men get down on to the Barrier next day, to Shambles Camp, where they dig up a frozen pony carcass for a feed of meat. Descending the Glacier has taken eleven days.

Shackleton had similar crises on the glacier descent – losing his way, running out of food, illness and injury. But not a death. He set off across the Barrier on 28 January. Scott is starting the long haul across the Barrier twenty-one days later in the season than Shackleton, on 18 February.

Shackleton made it home on the last day of February. Just surviving. The Barrier in February is beginning to be a very cold and unforgiving place. Almost exactly a year ago Scott turned back on the Barrier from his effort to put the big One Ton Depot at 80 degrees south, because the harsh conditions were too much for his ponies. Even travelling at Shackleton's rate, Scott now can't be home till near the end of March.

It's difficult to know when things go finally wrong. Little Birdie Bowers, eager, loyal, optimistic, strong, stops writing his chatty diary entries at the top of the Glacier. Dr Bill Wilson, who kept detailed journals through both Antarctic trips, stopped writing nine days into the Barrier journey. Titus Oates had already stopped.

Some days they struggle for more than nine hours to travel six or seven miles. It's not nearly enough. Scott can force the pace no longer. They are deeply exhausted. Hungry. Thirsty. Weakening. Critically, they are short of fuel. Fuel is vital. They need it for cooking, for melting water to drink, to bring a little warmth in the tent.

The temperature drops. It's frighteningly, unexpectedly cold, and stays cold. In their weakened state the cold bores into their beings. The wind eases and they don't get the help they expected from their sledge sail. Worse, the sledge runners stick. The snow surface is like sandpaper. The weight they drag – although much lighter than before – is exhaustingly heavy. They are taking two times longer to cover each mile.

The lateness of the season becomes ominous.

On 15 March they've been on the Barrier for three-and-a-half weeks. There are still another 150 miles to go. It's bitterly cold, bleak, grey. Titus Oates is in agony. He cannot pull the sledge. His feet are frostbitten, now they are gangrenous. The old wound in his thigh hurts appallingly. Scurvy can cause wounds not to heal, old wounds to reopen. Nobody mentions scurvy but Oates is almost certainly suffering from it.

Oates hopes that he will die in the night. He doesn't. He knows he's hindering the others. Probably on the morning of 17 March, his thirty-second birthday – but they were losing track of dates – he pushes out of the tent into the snow and limps away. Everyone knows what he is doing. No one follows.

The three remaining men struggle on for a couple more days. Scott is convinced they will never make it. His right foot is suddenly frostbitten. Gangrene threatens. That means amputation, Scott notes in his diary. He writes that Wilson and Bowers still think they'll get through. On 19 March they camp about eleven miles from One Ton Depot.

If only a year ago they had built the Depot at 80 degrees south, as they planned; then they would already have reached its supplies of food and fuel.

If only. There are so many if onlys. If only a blizzard hadn't begun, lifting the fine snow of the Barrier and blowing it along, like a running river over the surface, so that they can't see to find their way to the Depot, with its one black flag. If only the route to the Depot had been marked.

They have a little food and fuel remaining. Wilson and Bowers prepare to set out for the Depot to bring supplies. They are still able to walk.

But they don't go. Perhaps Scott thinks it's better to remain in the tent, to be found together, better for their diaries and records to be in one place. Beyond One Ton there are still another hundred miles to manage before they reach safety.

So they lie in the tent in their sleeping bags, day

after day, while the snow drifts outside, and the wi...
blows, and their food runs out, and their fuel finishes.
They write their last letters home, brave, loving
letters. 'It is only sleep in the cold,' writes Bowers to
his mother.

Scott has kept his diary going nearly to the end,
providing the record for future readers. Now he
writes movingly of their last days. Or hours. No one
knows. No one knows when each man finally dies,
out on the Barrier, while the snow drifts around
their tent, in the silence.

Chapter 20

THE WHOLE WORLD HAS NOW BEEN DISCOVERED

B ACK at Cape Evans, men wait.

The last support party – Teddy Evans, Lashley and Crean – arrive at Hut Point on 22 February, after a terrible journey from the plateau. Evans began to sicken with scurvy after only three weeks. He struggled on for another three weeks while Crean and Lashley hauled the sledge; he could only walk beside it. Then he collapsed. Crean and Lashley tied him to the sledge and dragged him along. Nearly at the end of the Barrier, Evans, now desperately ill, could go no further. Lashley nursed him while Crean marched eighteen hours non-stop, with only a little chocolate and a few biscuits for food, to get help, staggering into Hut Point delirious with exhaustion.

Evans, Crean and Lashley report that they left Scott and his team close to the Pole. So – judging by the time they needed for the journey back – they reckon Scott could arrive around the end of the first week in March. Scott has a team of five. Evans made it with just two men pulling the sledge much of the way.

On 25 February Cherry-Garrard sets out across the Barrier with two dog sledges, and Dimitri Gerov the Russian dog driver. Cherry doesn't understand how to drive dogs, or navigate, but no one else is available to go. As the temperature drops his glasses freeze up, so he can't see. But he gets to One Ton Depot and waits, ready to help the southern party when they appear out of the gloom.

It's bitterly cold, the dogs rapidly lose condition, their food begins to run short. Cherry wants to go further south. But that would be strictly against his orders. On 10 March, in miserable cold, the dogs frostbitten and thin, he turns back, deeply disappointed. He'd hoped to welcome the returning explorers with food and assistance.

Back at Cape Evans no one is yet feeling

anxious that Scott has not arrived.

The *Terra Nova* has already departed, heading north, away from the gathering ice. There is no news to take home. Nobody knows whether Scott got to the Pole, or Amundsen, or when Scott will return.

On 7 March 1912 after a long stormy voyage from Antarctica, *Fram* reaches Hobart, Tasmania, arriving out of the Antarctic ahead of *Terra Nova*. Amundsen telegraphs the news of his victory. He is first at the South Pole. He has won. 'The whole world,' says the New York Times, 'has now been discovered.'

At Cape Evans winter comes, with darkness and isolation. Now the men left behind in the hut know that their companions must be dead. They talk about what could have happened. Cherry-Garrard thinks they all fell into a crevasse. Lashley believes they died of scurvy.

As soon as they can travel the following summer a search party sets out south, departing on 20 October 1912. They take a dog team, and Himalayan mules ordered by Oates and delivered by *Terra Nova*.

In two weeks, eleven miles beyond One Ton, they see a single bamboo sticking up out of a mound of snow, and discover the tent, drifted up. The leader of the search party is a naval doctor. He crawls inside and finds the frozen bodies of Scott, Wilson and Bowers. The cold preserves perfectly: the men are as they died. He gathers the search party and, standing on the Barrier, silent sad men, he reads the final pages of Scott's diary. And so, at last, they hear that their companions did get to the Pole. And – what the rest of the world has known for seven months – that the British were second.

They leave the bodies of Scott, Wilson and Bowers where they were found, out on the Barrier, with the tent collapsed over them, and a cairn of snow piled on top with a cross made of Tryggve Gran's skis. They look south for Oates' body. Failing to find it, they build another cairn and cross.

Amongst the things taken back to the hut at Cape Evans are a small camera and two rolls of film. The film has been dragged on a sledge to the Pole, and nearly back again. It has lain out on the Barrier in the deep cold of the Antarctic winter for eight months. One of the scientists decides to try developing it. The chance of seeing anything seems very small.

But there, astonishingly, are images. Five weary

faces stare out. Commemorating the achievement of the Pole. Scott, Wilson, Evans, Oates, Bowers. The slight movement of Bower's hand can just be seen, as he pulls the string attached to the camera shutter.

And there is another photograph. A photograph of a small dark tent, securely pegged into the snow, Norwegian flag fluttering. The tent put up by Roald Amundsen and his men. First at the South Pole.

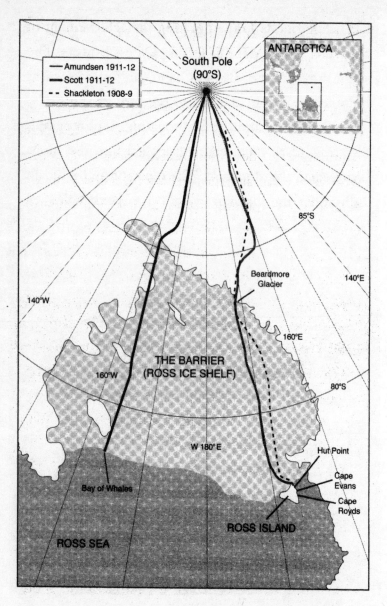

This map shows the routes taken by Shackleton, Amundsen and Scott.

WHAT HAPPENED AFTERWARDS

Amundsen had got to the South Pole first.

In Britain, there was disbelief, indignation. Amundsen was described as a professional, as a man who sneaked in and sprinted for the Pole. Scott was described as wanting to do important scientific work; the Pole was only part of his plans. Racing wasn't intended. Amundsen's achievement was admired, but there was no discussion about why he had got there first. Scott, it was said, had experienced bad weather, bad luck. That was why he hadn't beaten Amundsen.

The last news of Scott was on 4 January 1912, as he set off with the final party from 87 degrees 32 minutes south, to travel 150 miles to the Pole. Nobody knew anything more.

But when the news broke in February 1913 of Scott's death and of his men's frozen bodies in the snow – it overwhelmed Amundsen's success. British failure became dramatic tragedy. Scott, and his men, were heroes.

Scott's diaries were edited for publication. Scott wrote eloquently, and persuasively. Amundsen's account was understated and straightforward by comparison. His professional approach to polar exploring was discounted. He was seen as 'unsporting'. The British were seen as glorious amateurs.

History is often written by the victors. But in Antarctica, the defeated seemed to win. The First World War began in 1914, with its appalling destruction of life. The ideals of sacrifice and devotion to one's country became all-important. Scott and his dead companions seemed to symbolise the young men killed in battle.

Amundsen was shattered by the death of Scott and his men. His voyage to the Arctic Sea in the *Fram* never happened; but he tried to achieve his long-dreamed-for drift across the Arctic Ocean in a new ice-ship, beginning in 1918.

Amundsen died some time in June 1928 aged fifty-six, when the aircraft he was flying in disappeared over the Polar Sea. He was searching for survivors of an attempt to fly to the North Pole in an airship.

Ernest Shackleton led a new expedition to the Antarctic in 1914. He wanted to be the first to walk across the continent, from one coast to the other, through the South Pole. His ship *Endurance* was trapped in the ice for many months before being crushed. After extraordinary adventures and amazing journeys, Shackleton managed to save all the men who had been with him on *Endurance* and bring them to safety.

Shackleton died in 1922 aged forty-seven on the way to Antarctica, during a third expedition.

No one managed to cross the Antarctic continent via the South Pole until the Commonwealth Trans-Antarctic Expedition of 1957-58.

ANTARCTIC EXPEDITIONS
IN THIS BOOK

British Naval Expedition
1839–43
Leader: James Clark Ross
Ships: *HMS Erebus, HMS Terror*
Place: Ross Sea
Farthest south: 78 degrees
10 minutes south

Belgian Antarctic Expedition
1897–1899
Leader: Adrien de Gerlache
Ship: *Belgica*
Place: Antarctic Peninsular

British Antarctic Expedition
1898–1900
Leader: Carsten Borchgrevink
Ship: *Southern Cross*
Base: Cape Adare, Antarctic
continent
Farthest south: 78 degrees
50 minutes south,
16 February 1900

British National Antarctic
Expedition 1901–04
Leader: Robert Falcon Scott
Ship: *Discovery*
Base: Hut Point, Ross Island
Farthest south: 82 degrees
17 minutes south,
30 December 1902

British Antarctic Expedition
1907–09
Leader: Ernest Shackleton
Ship: *Nimrod*
Base: Cape Royds, Ross Island
Farthest south: 88 degrees
23 minutes south, 9 January
1909

Norwegian Antarctic Expedition
1910–12
Leader: Roald Amundsen
Ship: *Fram*
Base: Bay of Whales, Ross Ice
Shelf
Farthest south: 90 degrees
south, the South Pole,
14 December 1911

British Antarctic Expedition
1910–13
Leader: Robert Falcon Scott
Ship: *Terra Nova*
Base: Cape Evans, Ross Island
Farthest south: 90 degrees
south, the South Pole,
17 January 1912

MEASURING DISTANCE

Latitude and Longitude

Two sets of invisible lines divide the surface of Earth. Lines of latitude run around the Earth in rings, each ring the same distance apart. Lines of longitude run up and down the Earth, between the North and South Poles, dividing the surface into segments, like an orange. The lines of latitude and longitude are divided up into 'degrees' and 'minutes'. Using this invisible network of lines it is possible to find out exactly where you are on the Earth's surface.

Latitude is measured from the equator, in degrees, represented by the symbol °. One degree south (1° S) is just below the equator. Ninety degrees south (90° S) is the South Pole, where all the lines of longitude come together and meet at the same point.

Nautical Miles

Each degree of latitude is divided into sixty parts, called 'minutes', represented by the symbol[1]. Each minute equals one nautical mile, so there are 60 nautical miles between one degree of latitude and the next.

Explorers trying to get to the South Pole knew that, for example, when they'd got to 89° S there were 60 nautical miles to go to the South Pole at 90° S.

SOME INFORMATION ABOUT ANTARCTICA

The Antarctic Continent

The Antarctic continent is the Earth's fifth largest continent, half as big again as the United States. It contains one tenth of all the planet's land mass. No one really knew the final shape of Antarctica until images taken by satellites orbiting the Earth in the 1960s were pieced together. Vast thick sheets of ice smother Antarctica, burying almost all the continent. On average, the ice is 2,300 metres thick, making Antarctica the world's highest continent. The ice in the ice sheets flows very, very slowly down towards the coasts.

The South Pole

The South Pole is high on the rounded plateau of central Antarctica, 2,793 metres above sea level. The ice covering the Pole is 2,653 metres deep. The temperature never rises to freezing point, even in summer when the sun does not set. The average temperature all through the year at the Pole is minus

49 degrees Celsius. There is darkness for six months of the year, and light for the other six months.

Today there is a United States base, the Amundsen-Scott Station, at the South Pole. A large stripey pole with a silver ball on top, surrounded by flags, celebrates the South Pole.

The position of the actual South Pole is marked by a small stripey pole, which moves slowly, as the mighty ice sheet it is hammered into slips towards the sea. The ice at the Pole moves about ten metres a year. The real South Pole does not move. So every year the small stripey pole must be re-positioned.

The Transantarctic Mountains

The Transantarctic Mountains are like a buttress, a dam wall, holding back the huge mass of ice in the enormous ice sheet that covers the centre of Antarctica. The mountains – one of the world's longest mountain chains – cross the continent from sea to sea, in an unbroken curve, rising from sea level to about 4,000 metres.

The Barrier – The Ross Ice Shelf

The ice of the great ice plain the explorers travelled over is an ice shelf, formed by the glaciers and ice streams flowing off the high central ice cap through the mountains. It is part of one of the great ice sheets that cover Antarctica. The triangle-shaped Ross Ice Shelf, bigger than France, is Antarctica's largest ice shelf. It is a desert. Nothing lives on it.

Scientists discovered in 1977–8 that the ice of the Ross Ice Shelf does indeed float on the sea. Ice shelves move slowly, endlessly. At their front edge, huge pieces break off and float away as icebergs. The ice where Amundsen built his hut Framheim did in fact break off some time after he left. Huge icebergs continue to calve from the Ross Ice Shelf. In March 2000, a 250 kilometre stretch of ice at the Bay of Whales broke away, forming a massive 11,000 square kilometre iceberg.

The Southern Ocean

The deep, stormy Southern Ocean completely surrounds Antarctica. Every winter, the surface of the sea freezes, until, by early spring, 18 million square kilometres of ice covers more than half the ocean. Even by late summer, one fifth of the ocean is still covered by ice.

Dogs

Dogs are no longer allowed on the Antarctic continent. Adventurers making long sledge journeys in Antarctica today man-haul their sledges, like early explorers used to do. The sledges are made of lightweight materials, aerodynamically designed.

Explorers' Health

Scurvy usually attacked explorers in Antarctica towards the end of expeditions, after months of eating dried or tinned food. In the early stages, scurvy made the sufferers feel cold, weak, slow, unable to concentrate – just when they needed all their strength to survive. It caused painful swollen joints, softened bones, loose teeth, bleeding, and – finally – death.

Gradually scientists realised that the dreadful disease scurvy was caused by vitamin deficiencies, in particular vitamin C that is found in some fresh fruit, vegetables, and in fresh meat.

Deficiencies of other vitamins can also affect people's behaviour and proper functioning.

When explorers were trying to get to the Pole, no one knew about the effects of dehydration – not drinking enough liquid. We now know that people working in the cold can easily get dehydrated, and need to drink a great deal. Dehydration can make people lose their ability to make good judgements, and affect the efficient functioning of their bodies.

Weather on the Barrier, February–March 1912

Measurements of temperature recorded by US automatic weather stations on the Ross Ice Shelf over a recent ten year period show that the persistent cold temperatures reported by Scott from late February to 19 March 1912 were exceptionally low. The remarkably cold temperatures would have contributed to the exhaustion and frostbite suffered by Scott and his companions. The intense cold would also have created difficult surface conditions, affecting the sliding of skis and the sledge runners.

A Comparison

On the journey to the South Pole, with dogs pulling the sledges, Amundsen and his men managed on average fifteen miles a day, which took them five to six hours.

Scott and his men man-hauled for up to ten hours a day, achieving on average ten to twelve miles, but expending much more energy.

Glossary

Altitude	the height of an object in relation to a given point (usually sea level).
Antarctic	the enormous region at the bottom of the world. The word usually refers to the continent and its islands, the ice and the surrounding ocean.
Arctic	the north polar regions.
Axis	an imaginary point around which an object rotates.
Blizzard	a blinding storm of wind and snow.
Cairn	a mound built as a monument or landmark.
Crampons	spiked iron plates fixed to boots for climbing or walking on ice.
Crevasse	a deep open crack in a glacier.
Depot	a store.
Dysentery	an infection of the intestines which causes severe pain and diarrhoea.
Frostbite	injury to body tissues caused by freezing.
Gabardine	a hard-wearing cotton cloth.
Gangrene	the decomposition of part of a living body.
Glacier	a mass of land-ice formed by a build-up of snow on high ground.
Herbivore	a plant-eating animal.
Hierarchy	a system of ranking, in order of importance.
Husky	a powerful breed of dog with thick fur, used for pulling sledges.

Ice floe	a piece of floating sea-ice whose edges can be seen.
Igloo	a dome-shaped house made of snow.
Latitude and longitude	see pages 4 and 111.
Man-hauling	a method by which humans, wearing a harness, pull supplies on sledges, instead of using animals such as dogs or horses.
Nautical miles	measurements of distance that relate to latitude and longitude, as used by sailors, pilots and explorers. One hundred nautical miles equals approximately 115 statute (or land) miles.
Navigator	someone who locates position during a journey.
Pemmican	a mixture of pre-cooked meat, dried and pounded, and mixed with melted fat.
Plateau	an area of level high ground.
Prototype	an original design from which copies can be made.
Scurvy	a disease caused by lack of vitamin C.
Snow-blindness	a painful temporary blindness caused by the glare of sunlight reflected on a large expanse of snow.
Statute mile	a linear measurement equal to 1.609 kilometres. This measurement is commonly used on land.

Index